PRAYING YOUR THORNS WITH THE MYSTICS

A STUDY GUIDE FOR

Chronic Grace:

Prayers, Saints, and Thorns That Stay

JULIE K. RHODES

Copyright 2024 by Julie K. Rhodes. *Praying Your Thorns with the Mystics: A Study Guide for Chronic Grace: Prayers, Saints, and Thorns That Stay*

All Rights Reserved
Published by Leadership Books, Inc. Las Vegas, NV – New York, NY
LeadershipBooks.com

ISBN:
978-1-951648-93-0 (Paperback)
978-1-951648-94-7 (eBook)

All Rights Reserved. No part of this publication may be reproduced, distributed, or transmitted in any form or by any means, including photocopying, recording, or other electronic or mechanical methods, without the prior written permission of the publisher, except in the case of brief quotations embodied in critical reviews and certain other noncommercial uses permitted by copyright law.

Leadership Books, Inc is committed to publishing works of quality and integrity. In that spirit, we are proud to offer this book to our readers; however, the story, the experiences, and the words are the author's alone. The conversations in the book all come from the author's recollections, not word-for-word transcripts. All of the events are true to the best of the author's memory. The author, in no way, represents any company, corporation, or brand mentioned herein. The views expressed are solely those of the author.

All Scripture quotations, unless otherwise indicated, are taken from the *Holy Bible, New International Version*®, NIV® Copyright ©1973, 1978, 1984, 2011 by Biblica, Inc.® Used by permission. All rights reserved worldwide.

TABLE OF CONTENTS

A Note from Julie 1

How to use this Guide 5

Group Guidelines 9

Week 1: Praying Your Grief of Before 11

Week 2: Praying Your Bewilderment with Ignatius 21

Week 3: Praying Your Restlessness with Augustine 31

Week 4: Praying Your Fear with Julian of Norwich 41

Week 5: Praying Your Hunger with Teresa of Avila 51

Week 6: Praying Your Stillness with Francis of Assisi 61

Other Resources 69

Bios 71

More *Chronic Grace* Resources 73

A NOTE FROM JULIE

This is a study guide through *Chronic Grace: Prayers, Saints, and Thorns That Stay*, a memoir I wrote about my struggle with Long Covid. It's kind of weird to have a study guide for a memoir, right? And yet here we are, looking cute and darling and holding it in our hands.

The focus of this particular study guide is the part of my book that deals with the mystics and how they prayed. When I was writing *Chronic Grace*, I was lonely writing all by myself and about myself, so I enlisted the help of some 500-year-old friends to beef things up and keep me company. Wow, did they teach me a lot about praying through my "thorn." They were merry, odd colleagues.

I hope you'll feel the same way when you are done with this guide.

I don't know what your thorn is, but you do. You know why you're holding this guide, why you maybe even read the original book itself. Thorns come in many flavors of bad: health issues, relational impasses, mental anguish. We pray and pray for their resolution, and all we hear is the sound of our own voice in a dark, vast room. This room feels like a hotel conference room, indifferent, our cries swallowed by acres of geometric carpet and movable walls.

The trouble of how to connect with God, especially in suffering, goes back a long way. Maybe you are familiar with some of the friends I'm roping into our discussion: Ignatius of Loyola, Augustine of Hippo, Julian of Norwich, Teresa of Avila, and Francis of Assisi. There's no way to thoroughly do each of them justice in a book or in a study guide, but I've tried to focus on what seems to me to be their particular "thing" and how that might apply to us thorn-bearers who are trying to pray at proverbial abandoned Marriots.

Ignatius was famous for his use of imaginative prayer, Augustine for his love of Scripture, Julian for her connection to the love of Jesus himself, Teresa to practical prayer practices, and Francis to a prayer life shaped by the cross. They had other "things" too, but these were my takeaways after reading some of their work and biographies. I'm certainly not claiming to be a scholar, just a student both of the mystics and of suffering itself. Not-so-incidentally, each of these mystics suffered long-term physical illnesses, so we are in (somewhat relatable) company.

In April of 2020, I was a healthy mom of two kids with a husband, a pug, and a professional acting career. I jogged four times a week. I sang and danced in shows. I was accustomed to embodying characters who started with a problem and finally found resolution, or at least a way forward, at the end of the story.

And then I got sick. And for the next year and a half, would be plagued with what my medical team ultimately decided must have been a long-term Covid infection, followed by a cancer scare and surgery that threatened my career and made symptoms worse.

How was I supposed to operate in this new category of normal?

How was I supposed to talk to God about something he clearly didn't see fit to stop?

These are the questions my memoir asks, and that hopefully this study guide might begin to answer in some small, though meaningful ways.

It is here I want to emphasize the word "guide." This is not a how-to manual to finally and fully make peace with your thorn, with God, or with yourself. This is more of an incidental opportunity for you to gather with other thorn-bearers and learn from each other, organically, led by the Spirit and Scripture to comfort and empower you in wildly specific ways.

I'm privileged to be a small part of that. I wish I could sit in on your group discussions, learn from you, and hear your thorn-ographies. Maybe someday.

Until then, know you are not alone.

Love,
Juls

HOW TO USE THIS GUIDE

Gathering a Group

This study guide is designed for a group setting, even if it's only a group of two! Thorns vary in type and sensitivity, so you might want a very small group of confidential members or a larger group that is dealing with the same type of issue. Decide what sort of group you would like to lead, and prayerfully invite members.

(This group could already exist as a Bible study group, therapy group, book club, etc.)

This study guide is broken up into six weeks, which correspond to the six chapters of *Chronic Grace*. A weekly meeting time is the most natural format, but certainly you can expand or contract as needed.

Each week's meeting is designed for a 90-minute group time. This allows some buffer for socializing and settling in for basically a two-hour get-together.

The study is designed to be used in conjunction with ***Praying Your Thorns with the Mystics: A Video Guide for Chronic Grace: Prayers, Saints, and Thorns That Stay.*** To purchase this course, visit leadershipbooks.com.

Format

Each session is divided into six parts, with a Prep section following each week for group members to complete on their own before the next gathering:

Read (2 minutes)
Group leader will have a member read the short Scripture passage and introduction provided.

Respond (10 minutes)
This is a brief group discussion time to get everyone warmed up to the topic and follow up on the Prep from the week before.

Watch (20 minutes)
Group leader will play the corresponding video for that week's lesson.

Ponder (30 minutes)
This is a longer group discussion time to dig deeper into the themes of the video.

Apply (15 minutes)
Group leader will have members reflect on the discussion and set their intentions for the week. Group members are invited to share how they intend to move forward with a new insight or tool.

Pray (10 minutes)
This is a time for group members to share more specific prayer requests and pray aloud. Julie has provided a closing prayer for a member to read aloud if desired.

Prep/Therapist Tip
This section provides a suggested reading from *Chronic Grace* for the week to come, and a question prompt to get members thinking

about the next week's theme in advance. Most importantly, this section offers a **Therapist Tip** for members to read, ponder, and apply. Licensed trauma therapist Andie McQuitty provides a short exercise that corresponds to the week's main theme. Along with the wisdom and inspiration of Scripture, the witness of church fathers and mothers, and the Spirit-led discussion of group members, a therapist will enhance the ways we tackle our thorns on a practical, week-to-week basis.

Video Access info

Need to purchase the video guide? Click the QR below:

GROUP GUIDELINES

The group leader should review this with all members ahead of time.

Sensitivity

Our thorns create tender places in our hearts. It takes a lot of courage to share something vulnerable or unflattering. Group members should each always commit herself or himself to gentleness.

Restraint

This is not a group designed to "fix" anyone's thorn. Group members should respect each other enough to believe they have already done everything in their power to improve the situation. This group is about learning prayer practice, not trying to fix each other, as well intentioned as the impulse can be.

Confidentiality

Our deepest hurts and hang-ups become exquisite gifts of trust when we carefully hand them to others. It is a severe breach of that trust to casually discuss another group member's thorns outside of the safety of the meeting time.

Respect

This study was written with the understanding that people of many backgrounds might want to participate in discussion. If the group is not homogenous in background or belief, please be discerning and respectful of one another. This is not a place to argue apologetics or theology. It's the author's hope that we all might be comfortable engaging mystery with humility.

Attendance

This guide builds on itself week-to-week, so it's important for group members to commit to attendance for the six sessions. Time is not built into the week's structure to catch up group members who have been absent. Please also commit to being punctual.

Distractions

Cell phones, restless babies, greasy fast-food dripping down your arm — none of these lend themselves to focusing the mind and heart on the group discussion. Please silence electronic devices and try to find a time and place to meet when childcare is most convenient for group members. Food and drinks are a wonderful part of any gathering but try to get that out of the way before you sit down together.

To Bring

Group members might want to bring a journal for extra notes. Other items to grab: your favorite Bible (NIV or ESV or The Message are probably most helpful), and a pen.

For an enhanced experience, group members should also have a copy of ***Chronic Grace: Prayers, Saints, and Thorns That Stay*** for reading between weeks.

WEEK 1

PRAYING YOUR GRIEF OF BEFORE

READ

Have a group member read the following section aloud (2 minutes):

"Therefore, in order to keep me from becoming conceited, I was given a thorn in my flesh, a messenger of Satan, to torment me. Three times I pleaded with the Lord to take it away from me. But he said to me, "My grace is sufficient for you, for my power is made perfect in weakness." Therefore I will boast all the more gladly about my weaknesses, so that Christ's power may rest on me."
2 Corinthians 12:7b-9

From Julie:

Hi, Friend. **So, what's your thorn?**

Have you ever been asked that? Probably not in that way.

But chances are, you have a thorn.

Look around at your life, your neighbor's life.

Maybe it's chronic illness. A chronically difficult relationship. Ongoing trauma, or continual guilt from the past. It's like a shadow cast across each beautiful, awful day.

In 2 Corinthians 12, the Apostle Paul tells his readers that a "thorn in his flesh" was given to him so that he might not become conceited about the great revelations God had given him.

Although Paul begs God to be rid of his thorn (whatever it was), Jesus tells him, "My grace is sufficient for you, for my power is made perfect in weakness."

A short, simple reply, really. No explanation of how long the thorn will last or when it might ultimately resolve or how he might be using it to further advance the kingdom. Jesus skirts all of that and serves up his *grace* as a reasonable answer to Paul's every other question.

Those of us with thorns know how easy it is to fixate on the thorn and dismiss the grace when we lack proper definitions. We don't give grace a chance, really. What is grace, after all?

RESPOND

Group Discussion Questions (10 minutes):

For any who would like to share, **what "thorn" are you dealing with in this season?**

_____

_____

_____

_____

What does "giving grace a chance" mean for you right now? What do you hope to gain from this study?

_____

_____

_____

_____

WATCH

Access the Video Guide and watch the talk by Julie for Week One (20 minutes).

Video Notes:

PONDER

Group Discussion Questions (30 minutes):

1. *Pre-thorn, what used to be "easy" for you? (What central loss are you grieving?)*

   _____
   _____

2. *Pre-thorn, what was your operating definition of God's "grace?" Has that changed?*

   _____
   _____

3. *Why is it sometimes difficult to stop and grieve our Before life?*

   _____
   _____

4. *How has your prayer life changed now that you're in the After of your thorn?*

   _____
   _____

5. *What do you think will be the most valuable aspect to studying how the mystics dealt with suffering and prayer?*

   _____
   _____

APPLY

Have group members set their personal intentions for the week ahead (15 minutes):

Members may write their answers to the following questions in the space provided. If there is time for group members to share, feel free!

1. What stands out to you? Something from the video, book, or group discussion? Let this one insight inform how you endure your thorn over the next few days. *This week, I will commit to:*

   _____
   _____
   _____
   _____
   _____

2. What intentions can you set based on 2 Corinthians 12:7-9? *This week, I will be formed by the truth that:*

   _____
   _____
   _____
   _____
   _____
   _____

PRAY

Feel free to have group members share prayer requests as time allows, and then close in prayer by reading aloud the prayer provided by Julie below (10 minutes):

Dear Father of Both the Befores and Afters,

You had no beginning, and you have no end. There are no Befores or Afters in your character or in your love. You have been, and always will be, the same steady current of goodness and true reality.

We don't understand our present circumstances. They have marked a hard break in our lives, and we struggle to gain our bearings. For now, we sit still and grieve. We stop, we Selah. Our old lives have stopped and now so must we.

We cry for what has been lost. We know that you do, too, for your compassions never fail. Let us grieve mindfully in your presence.

We commit ourselves to you.

Amen.

Remember that group members should do the "Prep" section on their own before the next meeting.

PREP

Reflect:

This Week's Therapist Tip with Andie McQuitty, LMFT, MCAP, EMDR:

If you are doing this study, it is likely that you are open to working through some hard things. You are open to facing some of the painful realities in life and the impact of those realities on our souls.

Before entering in and engaging our feelings, it is most important to identify our reality. When we go through difficult circumstances in life, we have one of three natural responses to those circumstances. The first response is denial. If you are in denial, I imagine you are exhausted. It takes a lot of energy to attempt to avoid pain or pedal past painful memories as fast as you can.

The second possible response is minimization. If you are actively minimizing your pain, it's likely that you're afraid to really break down. You may be concerned about being "dramatic" or "acting like a victim," so you do your best to water down your description of your internal struggle.

The last option is acceptance. I like to define acceptance as the act of honoring myself and my situation. In acceptance, I look at my circumstances in the eyes, I link arms with the corresponding emotions and I face the thing head on.

Before we move forward on this journey together, will you honor yourself and take a moment to evaluate your response? Are you in denial? Are you minimizing your situation? Have you entered into the realm of acceptance?

As you evaluate, write or voice record your thoughts with no filter. After this, ask yourself, "Am I ready to move into the acceptance phase of healing?" If so, we have some hard and beautiful work ahead of us.

Read:

For a richer experience at the next group discussion, **read Chapter 2** of *Chronic Grace* beforehand.

Respond:

Why is the limbo of my "thorn" so bewildering?

_____

_____

_____

_____

_____

_____

_____

_____

_____

_____

_____

_____

_____

WEEK 2

PRAYING YOUR BEWILDERMENT WITH IGNATIUS

READ

Have a group member read the following section aloud (2 minutes):

"But my eyes are fixed on you, O Sovereign Lord; in you I take refuge — do not give me over to death."
– Psalm 141:8

From Julie:

My thorn arrived on a beautiful day, on the brightest and best of holidays. I was surrounded by goodness, by gifts, by God himself, and then — I couldn't get out of bed. No one would know what to do for months and months and months.

How was I supposed to live in this weird, new normal? I was utterly bewildered.

Living in limbo is unsettling, dizzying, adrenaline-reliant. It's a fight-or-flight life, where you never know what might happen — or not happen — next. Bewilderment is a no-man's land, a not-so-fun-house, a walk across ice.

Bewilderment can strike at any time. Before the grief, after the grief, even after we've achieved some level of thorn acceptance.

Being in the limbo of bewilderment demands we scramble for sure footing. It demands we spot a Fixed Star on a rough sea. There's no living with it otherwise.

RESPOND

Group Discussion Questions (10 minutes):

From this week's Prep: **why is the limbo of a thorn so bewildering?**

_____

_____

_____

_____

_____

_____

_____

_____

From this week's Prep: Andie says we are typically in denial, minimization, or acceptance of our thorn. Were you able to identify which of these natural responses you're currently inhabiting?

_____

_____

_____

_____

_____

_____

_____

WATCH

Access the Video Guide and watch the talk by Julie for Week Two. (20 minutes).

Video Notes:

PONDER

Group Discussion Questions (30 minutes):

1. *The point of Ignatius' Spiritual Exercises was to help people order their affections appropriately. What would you say is at the top of your list today?*

   _____

   _____

2. *Would you say you find yourself more in Consolation or Desolation most days?*

   _____

   _____

3. *Were there spiritual practices you wish you had adopted before your thorn set in?*

   _____

   _____

4. *What is the most helpful metaphor you can imagine for the good, all-encompassing sovereignty of God?*

   _____

   _____

   _____

APPLY

Have group members set their personal intentions for the week ahead (15 minutes):

Members may write their answers to the following questions in the space provided. If there is time for group members to share, feel free!

1. What stands out to you? Something from the video, book, or group discussion? Let this one insight inform how you endure your thorn over the next few days. *This week, I will commit to:*

   _____

   _____

   _____

   _____

   _____

2. What intentions can you set based on *Psalm 141:8*? *This week, I will be formed by the truth that:*

   _____

   _____

   _____

   _____

   _____

   _____

PRAY

Feel free to have group members share prayer requests as time allows, and then close in prayer by reading aloud the prayer provided by Julie below (10 minutes):

Dear God,

We want you to be our First Thing, the relationship of all relationships, the love above all loves, the attainment above all attainments. And yet, we feel off-balance in the limbo of our thorn. We want you, yes, but sometimes we want our lives back even more.

We focus our minds and hearts on your beauty right now, specifically the mysterious beauty of your total rule. We don't understand why, in your sovereignty, we are hurting. But just to know you know all, see all, and keep all in your jurisdiction, helps us to endure another day.

Let our imaginations be a place to practice your loving, overseeing presence today.

Amen.

Remember that group members should do the "Prep" section on their own before the next meeting.

PREP

Reflect:

This Week's Therapist Tip with Andie McQuitty, LMFT, MCAP, EMDR:

Engaging the imagination and ultimately gaining control over what happens in your mind is a discipline that takes practice. It is a skill. Like any skill, the more we use it, the more natural it feels.

I want to give you a few ideas for implementing this new skill. One of the most effective ways to engage the mind and settle into an image or a scene is to awaken all of our senses. As we experience life, we do it as a whole person: Spirit, Soul and Body. With imagery, we naturally engage the soul — our will, our mind and our emotions. We do not AS naturally engage the body. But when we learn to do so, we give ourselves a wider door to enter the places we imagine. Let's talk about what this looks like. Follow along with me.

I'd like you to identify a physical place where you meet with God. This place can be real or imagined. Once you pick the place, imagine that you are looking around. What are some things that you see with your eyes? (List them out loud.) Next, what does the air in this place feel like on your skin? Is there a cool breeze? Warmth from the sun? Imagine what it feels like to touch the air in this meeting place. Take a deep breath through your nose. What does it smell like? As you settle in, what are some of the sounds that you hear in your meeting place? As you engage all of your senses, your imaginative experience comes to life.

Read:

For a richer experience at the next group discussion, **read Chapter 3** of *Chronic Grace*.

Respond:

How does the emotion of restlessness manifest in your body?

WEEK 3

PRAYING YOUR RESTLESSNESS WITH AUGUSTINE

READ

Have a group member read the following section aloud (2 minutes):

"Why, Lord, do you stand far off?
Why do you hide yourself in times of trouble?"
Psalm 10:1-2

From Julie:

Sometimes it's hard to know the difference between struggling appropriately against bad things and rebelling against God. Maybe you can do a little of both at the same time.

As the months wore on and no doctor, medication, essential oil, or supplement seemed to fix my thorn, I grew more and more frustrated, determined, and obsessive.

I was restless, and I wanted God to be restless, too, on my behalf. Was that too much to ask?

Fortunately for us, the Psalms are filled with restless/rebellious prayers. What a mercy of God to include them in his official Book to affirm our very real, human emotions in times we don't understand and cannot fix.

The Lord's Prayer is also an anchoring framework for us, and can help us process the fidgety energy of restlessness. The prayer Jesus taught is like a bare bones skeleton we can flesh out with the muscle and blood of our own words.

To sum up: it helps to borrow the words OF Scripture in our prayers, and also to receive permission FROM Scripture to use words of our own.

RESPOND

Group Discussion Questions (10 minutes):

From this week's Prep: **How does the emotion of Restlessness manifest in your body?**

_____

_____

_____

_____

From this week's Prep: Andie challenged us to imagine a meeting place with God — what it feels like, smells, like, looks like. Would anyone like to describe what he or she imagined?

_____

_____

_____

_____

_____

WATCH

Access the Video Guide and watch the talk by Julie for Week Three. (20 minutes).

Video Notes:

PONDER

Group Discussion Questions (30 minutes):

1. *Do you agree that the opposite of anxiety is humility?*

2. *Have you ever found it hard to sit down with a Bible and keep an open mind? (Especially when you're restless?)*

3. *Have you ever had a real-time interaction with God through Scripture before? What characterized that experience?*

4. *Is there any part of The Lord's Prayer that you find difficult to pray in this season? Why?*

APPLY

Have group members set their personal intentions for the week ahead (15 minutes):

Members may write their answers to the following questions in the space provided. If there is time for group members to share, feel free!

1. What stands out to you? Something from the video, book, or group discussion? Let this one insight inform how you endure your thorn over the next few days. *This week, I will commit to:*

   _____
   _____
   _____
   _____
   _____

2. What intentions can you set based on *Psalm 10:1-2*? *This week, I will be formed by the truth that:*

   _____
   _____
   _____
   _____
   _____
   _____

PRAY

Feel free to have group members share prayer requests as time allows, and then close in prayer by reading aloud the prayer provided by Julie below (10 minutes):

Father in Heaven,

You understand. Thank you. You are familiar with palpitating hearts, tension headaches, knotted-up backs. Thank you. You see how our restless anxiety tries to warn and protect us, and you see when it no longer becomes helpful to us as we endure our thorns. Thank you. Being seen and known helps us to breathe.

Thank you for your Book, and for including all the frightening emotions we express when our confidence in You is shaken. What a dignifying, tender act. You include our perspective in the story of your work in the world, and this helps us to feel seen and heard. Thank you.

Bless us as we quiet ourselves before you and before your Words to us. We want to see and hear you now.

Amen.

Remember that group members should do the "Prep" section on their own before the next meeting.

PREP

Reflect:

> This Week's Therapist Tip with Andie McQuitty,
> LMFT, MCAP, EMDR:

I once had a client describe her anxiety as, "the motor in my chest." Another described his experience as, "the constant feeling of being in a small space." To another, "The thing that rises and falls, but is always there on some level."

Anxiety, fear, restlessness, feelings of being overwhelmed — they can all feel inescapable. One of the most difficult things for people is that sometimes answers or diagnoses don't come with the peace they thought it would. Sometimes an explanation or even just a rational thought leaves the person feeling even MORE overwhelmed than before.

Restlessness comes when we have so many thoughts, ideas and feelings that just will not organize themselves. Pausing can be a real challenge in this state of mind. I'd like to offer a new way to pause if this is your experience.

We are going to need two chairs. Yes, two. Place the two chairs across from each other, facing each other. Sit in one of the chairs, pause for just a second, take a breath and start talking to whoever you need that empty chair to represent. Unfiltered. This is a "word vomit" of sorts that may feel like it makes no sense at all. It is just a raw expression of your stream of consciousness with absolutely no judgment invited. At the end of the day, this is just a fancy way of "getting it out." All of those thoughts, feelings, and memories that just seem to bounce around like a bunch of ping pong balls in a bathtub? It's their time to bounce around. Just let them come.

Once you've done this, your capacity to pause will increase. Your unfiltered release provides the opportunity to pivot to a new mindset. This is a canal that feels a little dirty but leads to an open sea.

Read:

For a richer experience at the next group discussion, **read Chapter 4** of *Chronic Grace*.

Respond:

What is the difference between anxiety and fear? Are there defining qualities of each?

_____

_____

_____

_____

_____

_____

_____

_____

_____

_____

WEEK 4

PRAYING YOUR FEAR WITH JULIAN OF NORWICH

READ

Have a group member read the following section aloud (2 minutes):

"For I am convinced that neither death nor life, neither angels nor demons, neither the present nor the future, nor any powers, neither height nor depth, nor anything else in all creation, will be able to separate us from the love of God that is in Christ Jesus our Lord."
Romans 8:38-39

From Julie:

"Hi, Mrs. Rhodes," the nurse began. "The genetic profile of your thyroid came back. Your biopsy is showing a 70% chance of cancer."

After her napalm dropped, I only heard about every other word, like "surgeon" and "radiation" and "ASAP."

I told the nurse: "I'm still running almost daily fevers. Couldn't we wait until I was over a few more of my pandemic symptoms before we took out a major organ?"

She advised me not to wait longer than three or four weeks.

When I hung up, it hit me: "maybe Cancer" takes precedence over "maybe COVID."

The ante had been upped unfairly, and without my permission. Fears were sneaking up from every dark corner: what about my kids? What about my husband? What about what was left of my career? How does a body deal with cancer and Long Covid?

Fear is opening the door to a pitch-black room and waiting to be punched in the gut by an unseen fist. Fear can be the strongest feeling a thorn creates.

RESPOND

Group Discussion Questions (10 minutes):

From this week's Prep: **What is the difference between anxiety and fear? Are there defining qualities of each?**

_____

_____

_____

_____

_____

From this week's Prep: Andie challenged us with the "chair exercise" — sitting across from an empty chair and giving ourselves permission for an unfiltered release of words, memories, and emotions. Did this exercise create a change in your perspective that day?

_____

_____

_____

_____

_____

WATCH

Access the Video Guide and watch the talk by Julie for Week Four. (20 minutes).

Video Notes:

PONDER

Group Discussion Questions (30 minutes):

1. *Do you think it is possible for anyone to truly be "ready" for a thorn?*

2. *Does prayer for you feel more like incantation or conversation?*

3. *In the video, Julie says, "The highest prayer, therefore, isn't for a good event or a good development or for a good item or a good healing — although those are all good things to pray for. The* highest *prayer is an encounter with Good Jesus. And then wanting more of him, even as I have him." Does this definition of grace contradict what you've believed in the past?*

4. *Why do you think God allows dryness in prayer sometimes? How could it be profitable for us, even in our fears?*

5. *In the video, Julie says,* "Prayer is always a returning to our belovedness in [Jesus]." *Does this definition of prayer counteract the power of fear in your heart?*

_____

_____

APPLY

Have group members set their personal intentions for the week ahead (15 minutes):

Members may write their answers to the following questions in the space provided. If there is time for group members to share, feel free!

1. What stands out to you? Something from the video, book, or group discussion? Let this one insight inform how you endure your thorn over the next few days. *This week, I will commit to:*

   _____

   _____

   _____

2. What intentions can you set based on Romans 8:38-39? *This week, I will be formed by the truth that:*

   _____

   _____

   _____

PRAY

Feel free to have group members share prayer requests as time allows, and then close in prayer by reading aloud the prayer provided by Julie below (10 minutes):

Dear Jesus,

You are goodness itself. You are grace itself.

We have you with us now, gathered with our group, whether we feel you or not. You don't need to be invited or asked to stay. Your presence is here. Always here. And so we welcome you with a reverent "hello."

Our thorns threaten all we love and all we are. Help us to focus on your face instead of the fear in this moment.

You love us wholly, and we are wholly in the very palm of your hand. Nothing will come that can separate us from You.

We return now to our belovedness in You.

Amen.

Remember that group members should do the "Prep" section on their own before the next meeting.

PREP

Reflect:

This Week's Therapist Tip with Andie McQuitty, LMFT, MCAP, EMDR:

A traumatic experience is anything that threatens your wellbeing or the wellbeing of a loved one. When people endure ongoing sickness, pain, disease, toxic relationships, or abuse, they experience trauma.

There are many ways in which trauma impacts the brain and the body. We don't have time or space to go into all of these details, but one important piece of information to note is the way that trauma impacts our ability to communicate our thoughts and feelings with words. In his book **The Body Keeps the Score***, Dr. Bessel van der Kolk explains that trauma can impact the brain in a similar way as a stroke. Just as a stroke can leave someone with an inability to express themselves verbally, trauma leaves a person with the inability to communicate thoughts and feelings effectively. This can make it hard to come up with the words to share with family, friends, or God.*

Now, this is not the way that it has to be forever (because there are many effective treatment approaches for trauma), but we do have to accept that this may be one of the limitations we experience. The suggestion here is to find a different way to communicate. A way without words to start.

Here are some ideas: draw or paint a picture, find a song that expresses how you feel, share a quote that you read that you relate to, circle feeling words on the "feeling wheel" (Google it), or when it comes to prayer — you can just sit. God doesn't need your words all strung together perfectly to understand you.

Read:

For a richer experience at the next group discussion, **read Chapter 5** of *Chronic Grace*.

Respond:

How would you define spiritual hunger?

WEEK 5

PRAYING YOUR HUNGER WITH TERESA OF AVILA

READ

Have a group member read the following section aloud (2 minutes):

"Give us this day our daily bread."
Matthew 6:11

From Julie:

After my surgery, I asked the nurse, "Can I have some water?"

And realized: I *said* it. With a voice I still had that worked well enough to ask a question.

And then consciousness surged in: I had survived. Nothing catastrophic had happened, and I at least had something of a voice to ask for a drink.

It would have to be enough for now. It would have to be a little meal to eat, a bite of something sweet and small to tide me over. There would be no *conversations* today. No humming. No singing. No answers about the Cancer or the Covid.

Just a soft whisper — either the promise of a feast or the place where I would stay.

Could crumbs like that sustain me?

Spiritual hunger seems to be a byproduct of humility. We are lowered in some way — emotionally, physically, socially — and suddenly we feel a hole in our spiritual stomachs. It gnaws at us, this need to find something substantial to chew up, swallow, and digest.

There are many ways to eat, as we all know, but not all sustenance is created equal. We look to our old comforts — sometimes even physical food — to sustain us, but thorns don't allow the old ways to have much success.

We must find something new to eat.

RESPOND

Group Discussion Questions (10 minutes):

From this week's Prep: **How would you define spiritual hunger?**

_____
_____
_____
_____

From this week's Prep: Andie offered some different ways of expressing our thoughts and feelings about our thorns other than using words alone. Did any of your experiences reveal or satisfy your spiritual hunger in some way?

_____
_____
_____
_____

WATCH

Access the Video Guide and watch the talk by Julie for Week Five. (20 minutes).

Video Notes:

_____

_____

_____

_____

_____

_____

_____

_____

_____

_____

_____

_____

_____

_____

_____

_____

_____

_____

_____

PONDER

Group Discussion Questions (30 minutes):

1. *Do you think there are reliable shortcuts to grace, to the experience of Jesus' presence? Why or why not?*

2. *Why might there be a connection between humility and spiritual hunger? Why could this be a real mechanism?*

3. *Do you have a place you can go to be alone and fill up with grace (Jesus' presence)? What is it and how often do you go?*

4. *Is there a particular method or practice for focusing on Jesus that seems to work best for you?*

5. *Teresa's advice to "realize we are ill" is a gentle reminder that we can't always keep up rigorous methods of spiritual practice when we have a thorn. Do you find yourself on either extreme of the spectrum*

— either more likely to push too hard or give up altogether — or somewhere in between?

_____

_____

APPLY

Have group members set their personal intentions for the week ahead (15 minutes):

Members may write their answers to the following questions in the space provided. If there is time for group members to share, feel free!

1. What stands out to you? Something from the video, book, or group discussion? Let this one insight inform how you endure your thorn over the next few days. *This week, I will commit to:*

   _____

   _____

   _____

2. What intentions can you set based on Matthew 6:11? *This week, I will be formed by the truth that:*

   _____

   _____

   _____

PRAY

Feel free to have group members share prayer requests as time allows, and then close in prayer by reading aloud the prayer provided by Julie below (10 minutes):

Dear Jesus,

You once called yourself the Bread of Life. The more we have of you, the more filled up, satisfied, empowered, and nourished we are. The better we can sleep. The better we can think. You are not a piece of candy or an appetizer. You are three square meals that keep us awake and alert to a life of meaning, purpose, and peace.

Show each of us specific, practical ways to focus on you. Help us to wisely assess our schedules, our personalities, and the limitations of our thorns to determine the most realistic spiritual disciplines that will fit us best and connect us to you most deeply.

Feed us as we focus.

Amen.

Remember that group members should do the "Prep" section on their own before the next meeting.

PREP

Reflect:

This Week's Therapist Tip with Andie McQuitty, LMFT, MCAP, EMDR:

You may remember from Week 1 when I spoke about denial, minimizing and acceptance. I've had clients move into the acceptance phase, or maybe the "realization" phase. Like every good client, they typically ask, "Ok, I accept this reality. Now what?"

Many people are concerned that they will develop a victim mentality or lose some of their strength if they fully realize their struggle, or as Julie refers to it, their "thorn." Can I suggest something? What if you sat in it for a minute? I don't mean wallowing or complaining. I mean actually giving yourself the space to feel what you need to feel. Think what you need to think. Pray what you need to pray. This is all necessary before you do what you need to do.

Our culture is obsessed with action steps. We love to be told what to do next. My clients don't typically love when they ask me what to do and I say something like, "I can't tell you what to do. I can help you sit and experience where you are."

In the solitude, in the sitting, there's also a releasing. You release your next step for now and just simply learn to sit in the uncomfortable space of no action. This might be a bold statement, but I think it's in this space that people can fully realize what their needs are.

Read:

For a richer experience at the next group discussion, **read Chapter 6** of *Chronic Grace*.

Respond:

Does the idea of holding still in your thorn scare you?

WEEK 6

PRAYING YOUR STILLNESS WITH FRANCIS OF ASSISI

READ

Have a group member read the following section aloud (2 minutes):

"He will wipe every tear from their eyes. There will be no more death or mourning or crying or pain, for the old order of things has passed away."
Revelation 21:4

From Julie:

A few months after surgery, I went for a walk.

We were in Angel Fire, NM, for Spring Break, but skiing was incompatible with my fatigue, shortness of breath and fevers, so I was alone.

I took my time, trudging slowly to save what little I had in the metabolic reserves.

I stopped, finally. I stood still. Out beyond me was the quiet grandeur of mountain peaks.

What descended on me then was not snow, but a freeing calm that wriggled off the weight on my shoulders.

It was simplicity, lightness, breath.

It was then I felt an invitation: to be a human being again, one who could take her body back down to bed carefully and with attention.

Spiritual stillness is blessedly not dependent upon the resolution of thorns. There can be flashes of curiosity, of focus. There can even be moments of joy and a glimpsed possibility for being of service to others — not just despite our struggles, but because of them.

Stillness is possible, even in a world God hasn't put right yet. Jesus shows us this himself by holding still on a cross.

RESPOND

Group Discussion Questions (10 minutes):

From this week's Prep: **Does the idea of holding still in your thorn scare you?**

From this week's Prep: Andie challenged us to sit still and feel what we need to feel, think what we need to think, and pray what we need to pray before we rush to do what we need to do. What was this experience like for you?

WATCH

Access the Video Guide and watch the talk by Julie for Week Six. (20 minutes).

Video Notes:

PONDER

Group Discussion Questions (30 minutes):

1. *How would you define spiritual stillness?*

2. *Do you think holding still in your thorn might lighten your spiritual shoulders somehow? Why or why not?*

3. *Does pondering Christ's suffering for you help you trust him with the secrets he is keeping about your own suffering? How might this affect the way you pray?*

4. *Even as you prayerfully work to eliminate your thorn, are you willing to accept it on some level today as Jesus accepted his cross? How might you leverage it to love and to serve others?*

5. *Julie said, 'Jesus didn't die just for dying's sake but to set up a new creation someday where 'every tear will be wiped away,' where all his children will see his face in a place so bright it*

doesn't need the sun." *How might this idea help to quiet your soul into stillness?*

_____

_____

APPLY

Have group members set their personal intentions for the week ahead (15 minutes):

Members may write their answers to the following questions in the space provided. If there is time for group members to share, feel free!

1. What stands out to you? Something from the video, book, or group discussion? Let this one insight inform how you endure your thorn over the next few days. *This week, I will commit to:*

   _____

   _____

   _____

2. What intentions can you set based on Revelation 21:4? *This week, I will be formed by the truth that:*

   _____

   _____

   _____

PRAY

Feel free to have group members share prayer requests as time allows, and then close in prayer by reading aloud the prayer provided by Julie below (10 minutes):

Dear Savior,

You held still for us, long enough for love to do its work. Help us to do the same. We relax our jaws, our backs, our fists. We focus on the staggering sacrifice you made of your own free will. You made it willingly it so we could look forward to a world without pain, with no separation between us and You and each other. Your thorn was worth it to you.

Open our eyes to ways we might consecrate our own thorns for the good of others. Show us practical, daily opportunities to channel our pain into acts of mercy or service. Increase our ability to listen more attentively and compassionately to the pain of others.

If we die with you, we will also be raised with you in a world without end.

Amen.

CLOSING WORDS FROM ANDIE

This Week's Therapist Tip with Andie McQuitty, LMFT, MCAP, EMDR:

I was in a team meeting with the other therapists in my practice one day and I brought up one of my clients for the team to discuss. She was depressed. I mean really depressed. She cried through our sessions, could hardly speak, couldn't drive herself, and hadn't been to a grocery store in a year. Her doctor and I worked together to help her and at one point he said, "We might just have to accept this as an immovable diagnosis." I never talked to him again.

I couldn't accept that for her. I processed the case with some of my colleagues and one of them asked me, "Have you heard of the happiness quotient?" I said no. She began to explain that research shows that we can actually increase our capacity for happiness (even in the midst of a struggle or difficult season) if we express gratitude and if we focus on helping another person in some way.

I then remembered Kaitlyn. She was a client I worked with previously who was wheelchair-bound due to a back injury. She spent a year in bed and became so depressed she was losing her will to live. One day she joined a church online. She saw that they had an "online campus," so she put her name in the chat. Long story short, she is now the primary contact for that church online. She talks to people. Prays with them. Cares for them. She's still in a wheelchair. She's still in a lot of pain, but wow. She's happy.

Here's my last tip: every day, write down something that you're grateful for. Help one person. The rest will follow.

OTHER RESOURCES

For more resources on processing trauma, chronic illness, or anxiety, check out this list of resources Andie recommends:

The Body Keeps the Score: *Brain, Mind, and Body in the Healing of Trauma* by Bessel van der Kolk, M.D.

Try Softer: *A Fresh Approach to Move Us out of Anxiety, Stress, and Survival Mode — and into a Life of Connection and Joy* by Aundi Kolber, MA, LPC

The Wisdom of Your Body: *Finding Healing, Wholeness, and Connection through Embodied Living* by Hillary L. McBride, PhD

For more resources on prayer practices and the saints and mystics:

Desiring God's Will: *Aligning Our Hearts with the Heart of God* by David G. Benner

Opening to God: *Lectio Divina and Life as Prayer* by David G. Benner

BIOS

Andie McQuitty, LMFT, MCAP, EMDR

Andie is the founder of New Seasons Counseling and a Licensed Marriage and Family Therapist in the state of Florida. Andie obtained her Masters Degree in Clinical Psychology from Palm Beach Atlantic University and currently holds a Masters Level Certified Addiction Professional certification. Andie has years of experience providing counseling to adults, adolescents, couples, and families. Andie is trained in EMDR (Eye Movement Desensitization and Reprocessing) therapy, and utilizes this approach to target unresolved trauma with her clients. Andie incorporates spiritual health into her work with her clients, and believes that counseling is a wonderful tool for experiencing healing of all kinds and developing practical solutions for life's problems. Andie utilizes a compassionate, honest approach with clients to help them process life events, overcome struggles, and reach personal goals. It is Andie's sincere desire to see each of her clients experience health, wholeness, and peace.

Julie K. Rhodes

Julie is a writer and actor in Texas, and the author of *Chronic Grace: Prayers, Saints, and Thorns That Stay,* a memoir about her physical and spiritual journey through Long Covid. Connect with her at juliekrhodes.com.

MORE CHRONIC GRACE RESOURCES

- Purchase *Chronic Grace* at chronicgracebook.com.

- Is your book club interested in reading *Chronic Grace*? Download Book Club Questions at juliekrhodes.com.

- Interested in having Julie speak at your event or meet with your group? Contact juliekrhodes@juliekrhodes.com, or visit leadershipbooks.com/pages/speakers-bureau.

- Follow Julie @juliekrhodes on Instagram, Facebook, and X.

- Join Julie's newsletter here:

www.ingramcontent.com/pod-product-compliance
Lightning Source LLC
Chambersburg PA
CBHW050043080526
44586CB00014B/1437